Coloring Book
for Relaxation and Fun

40 Different Designs to color:
Ages 3 and up

Thank you for purchasing this coloring book.

For centuries coloring has been used for healing therapy purposes, to reduce anger, anxiety, to relieve everyday stress and feel calm. It can also be used to help in with
concentration.
The pictures can be colored by all ages.

In this coloring book you will find dragons, dinosaurs, elephants animals, flowers, mandalas and many more designs. Many people meditate on mandala designs.

Coloring puts you in the moment as if nothing else matters. Watching your designs come to life is so amazing.

On this page you will notice the names of some colors, what it promotes and when to use them.

   You do not have to use this color but go with your gut feeling as to which colors you feel comfortable with.

This is just a guide.

RED: Promotes...Energy, strength, motivation, desire, courage
   Use this color when you to give yourself a lift up and when you need courage.

ORANGE: Promotes...success, happiness, encouragement
   Use when you are feeling down and emotionally slumped.

GOLD: Promotes creativity, balancing thoughts and feelings, wisdom
   Use for depression, stress, anxiety.

YELLOW: Promotes...Uplifting, cleansing, joy, happiness
   Use for combating stress and lifting your spirits.

GREEN: Promotes...Balance, harmony, growth, stability,
   clear thinking.
   Use for   Stress, anxiety, depression and harmony.

TURQUOISE: Promotes... Calm, cleansing, healing, and friendly
   Use for stress, anxiety, anger.

Dark BLUE: Promotes...Calm, peace, relaxation, wisdom, creativity
   Use for, stress, anxiety, healing and calms you.

INDIGO: Promotes: Wisdom, intuition, spirituality, peace, calm, inspiration
   Use to combat anger and anxiety.

VIOLET / PURPLE: Promotes... Inspiration, imagination, wisdom, creativity,
   Use for awareness and spiritual fulfillment and peace.

Magnetta: Promotes... harmony and balance in every part of your life,
   and strengthens intuition.
   Use to strength contact with life purpose.

White: Promotes harmony, balance and healing
   Use for meditation, healing and spirituality.

PINK: Promotes...Calm, clarity of thought, affection, compassion.
   Use when you need to calm down and feel peace.

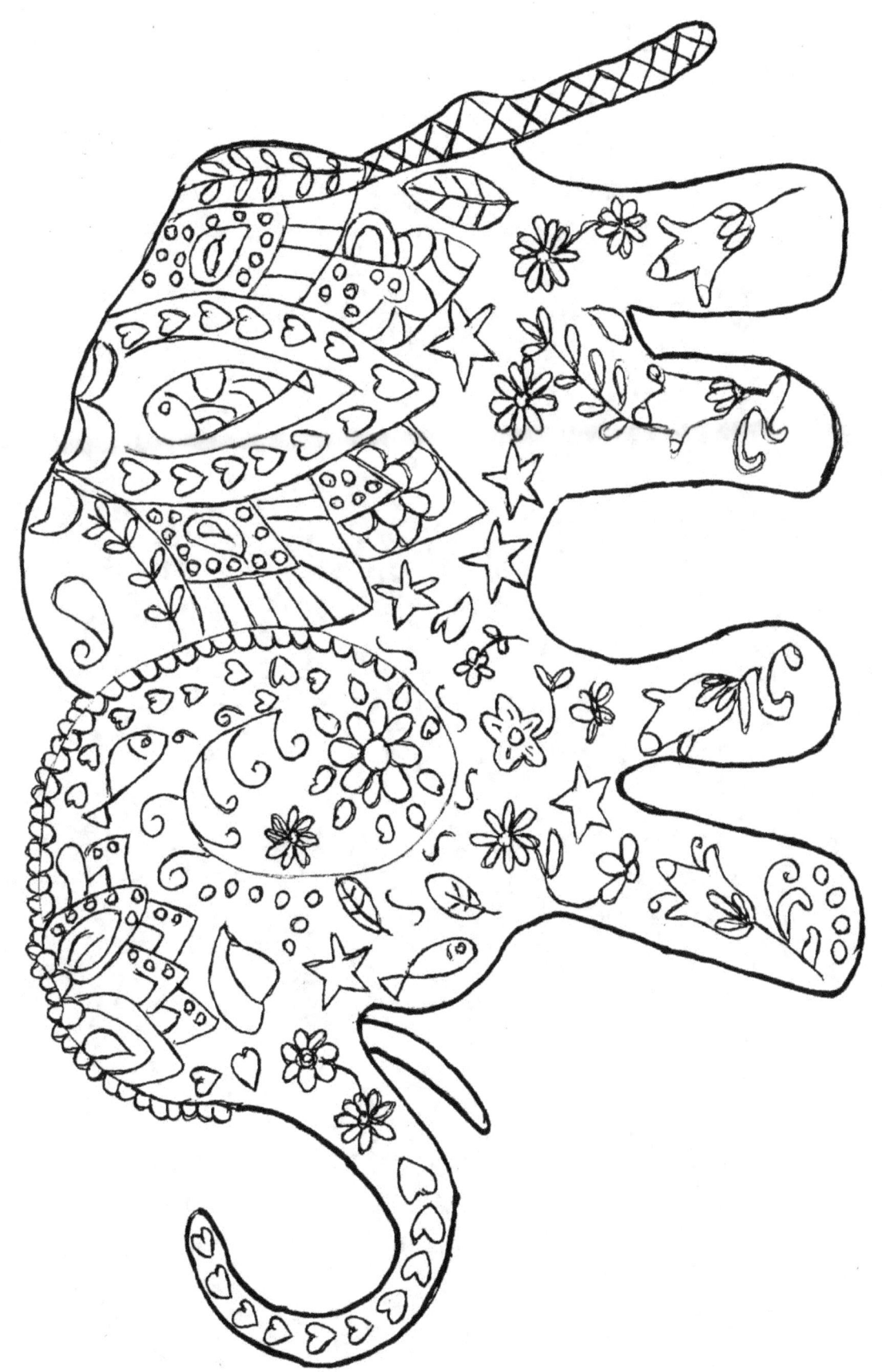

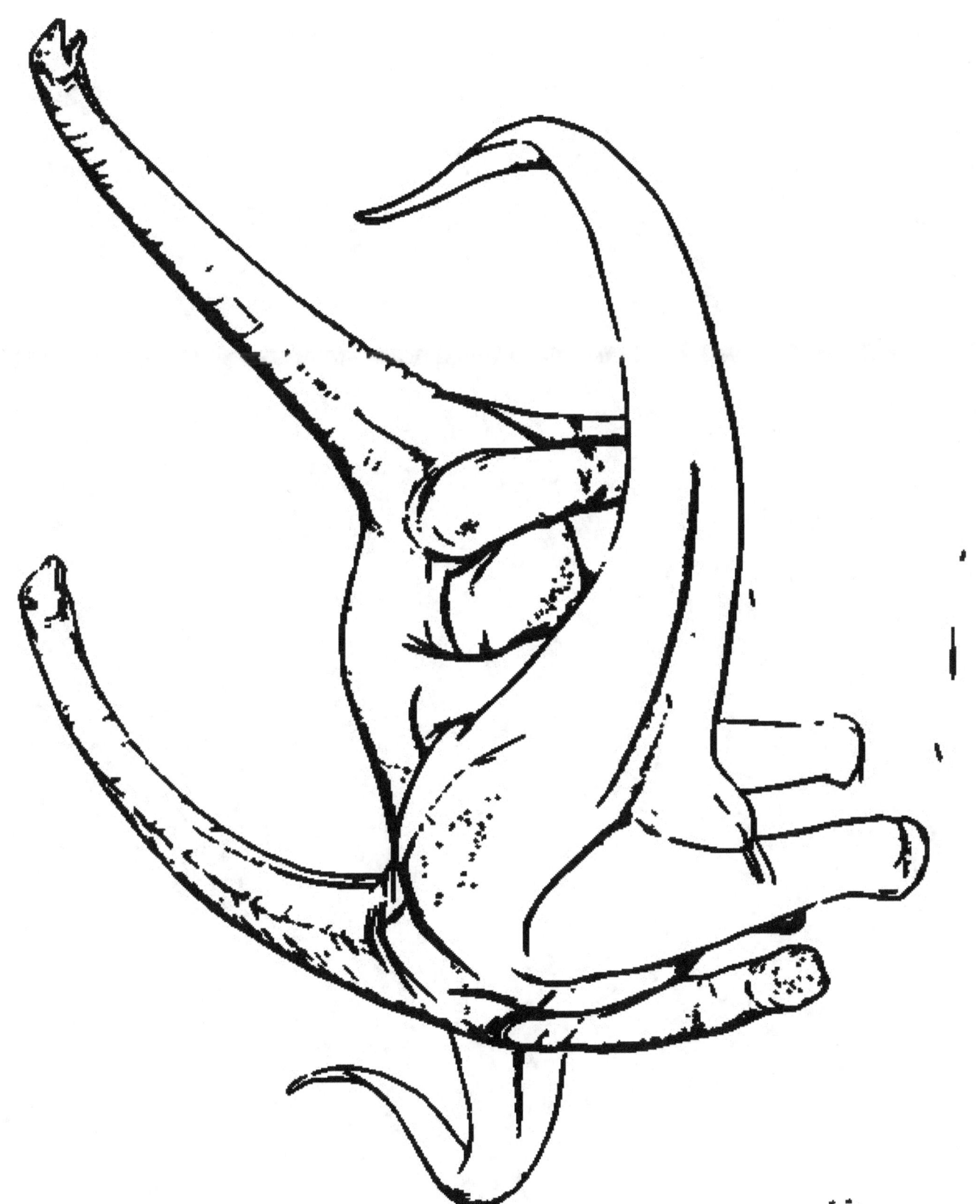

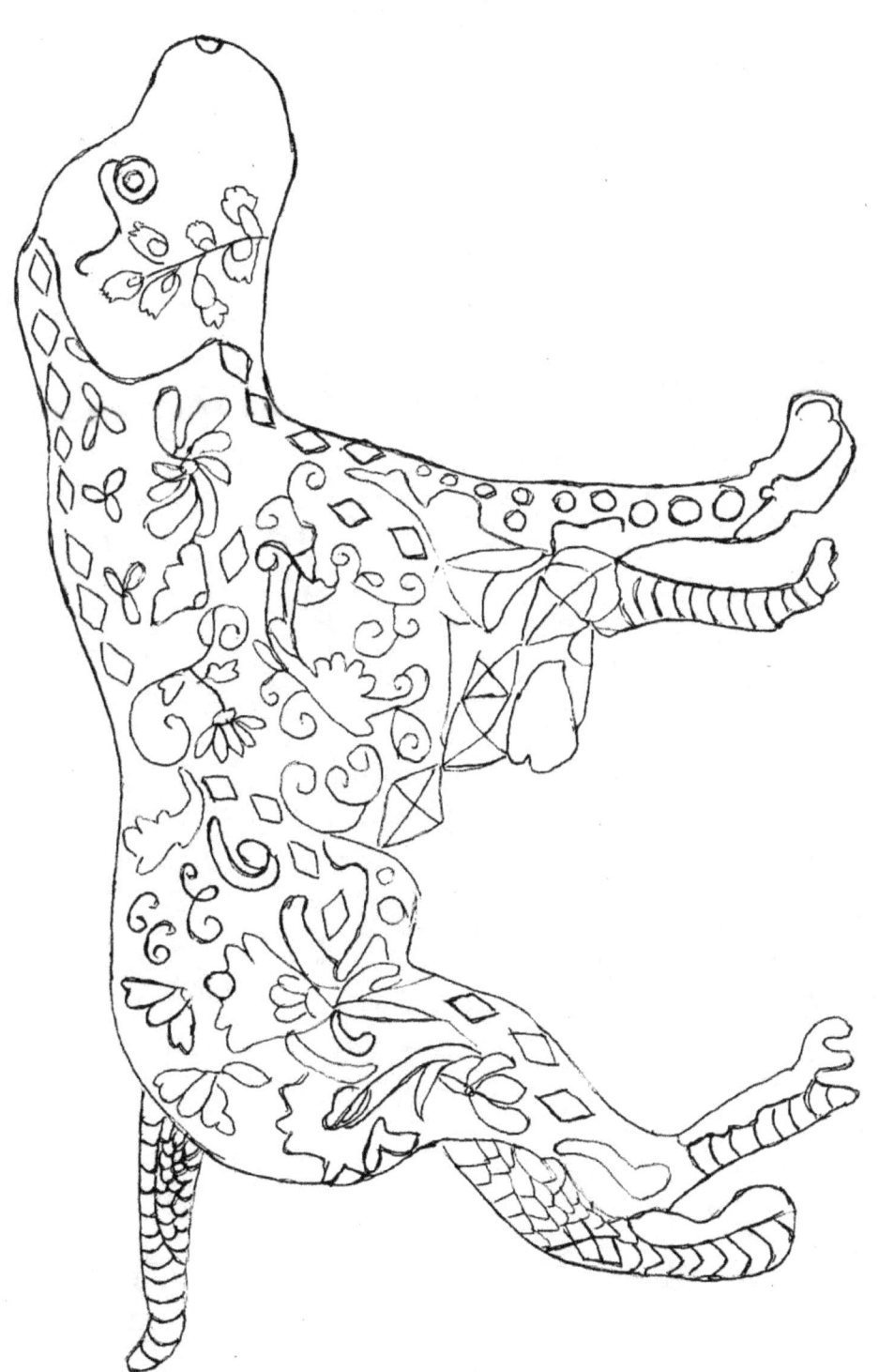

www.ingramcontent.com/pod-product-compliance
Lightning Source LLC
Chambersburg PA
CBHW081231280526
45787CB00006B/2619